Born Naughty

My Childhood in China

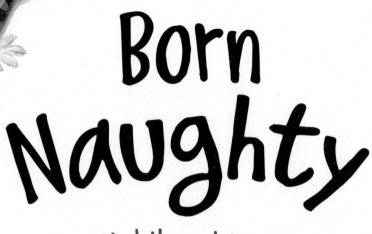

Jin Wang with **Tony Johnston**

illustrated by **Anisi Baigude**

a·s·b
anne schwartz books

Visit us on the Web! rhcbooks.com

Educators and librarians, for a variety of teaching tools, visit us at
RHTeachersLibrarians.com

Library of Congress Cataloging-in-Publication Data is available upon request.
ISBN 978-0-593-56361-8 (trade) — ISBN 978-0-593-56362-5 (lib. bdg.) —
ISBN 978-0-593-56363-2 (ebook)

The text of this book is set in 13-point Chronicle Text G1 Roman.
The illustrations were rendered in black ink and pencil.
Book design by Monique Razzouk

Printed in the United States of America
10 9 8 7 6 5 4 3 2 1
First Edition

For my mom, Su Qing Wang,
who raised me
and has always stood beside me.
—J.W.

For Jin.
Like bamboo, she does not bend.
—T.J.

For my *eej* and *aav*, Nabuqi and Huricha.
Your guidance and teachings are
my most prized treasures.
—A.B.

CONTENTS

THE BIGNESS OF WATER . . . 1

WATER ADVENTURE . . . 8

THE WILDNESS OF WIND . . . 16

POTATO MOUNTAIN . . . 20

A WALK WITH WOLVES . . . 24

TREE IN TROUBLE . . . 30

WINGS . . . 36

BIG RAIN, SMALL RAIN . . . 39

GIFT FROM THE STORM . . . 46

THE POPCORN MAN . . . 51

SCREAMING CHALK AND
SMOKE, SMOKE, SMOKE . . . 57

BLACK JUICE . . . 63

FAMILY PORTRAIT . . . 69

TINY HOUSE IN WINTER . . . 75

THE TASTE OF WINTER . . . 80

BRICKS AND LOVE . . . 83

GOOD FORTUNE . . . 89

AUTHORS' AND ILLUSTRATOR'S NOTES . . . 101

THE BIGNESS OF WATER

When I was young, I lived with my family in a mud house so tiny we barely fit inside. Our house had just one room, filled mostly with the bed we all shared—my mother, Ma, Diē (meaning "father"), my two younger brothers, and I. In this small space, we ran into each other all the time.

Our village, Nan Ba Zi, was in Inner Mongolia, part of China. It was so little it was not even on a map. It had about eighteen houses close together, and a tiny store where we could buy things like

soy sauce, salt, and matches. My village was beautiful. The clouds so pretty. The sky so blue.

On one side Nan Ba Zi was touched by a desert whose name I did not know. I never saw the desert, but I felt the sting of its sand in the time of wind. On the other side of the village, low hills, scattered with bushes and grass, watched over us.

To earn more money than he could in our village, Diē worked in a far place, making bamboo

steamers for cooking food. Except for rare times
when work was slow, he was not home until the
New Year came.

Because we had so little of it, water was a big,
big thing.

To save it, my family drank hardly any. Ma set
most aside for cooking and washing clothes. We
took baths once, maybe twice, a year and shared
about three cups of water each day for washing hands. I let my hands get very dirty before I

washed them. But—Ma's big rule—always before we ate we *had to* wash our hands.

All our family, but mostly Diē's father, Grand-father Zhao, who lived near us in a house even tinier than ours, was always thinking about water. He longed to see the great bigness of waters he had heard of, the big waters of the sea. So I called him Grandfather Ocean.

He was short, thin, a bit bent. When he smiled, his eyes looked like skinny moons. When he spoke, his voice was soft and slow. So wise, so calm, he brought calmness to everything.

In our village many people had two names. One that everybody *but* family used, and a spe-cial one that *only* family called you. Grandfather Ocean was in charge of giving us our special names. Of course, they were about water.

My first brother, six years old, was Haijun, meaning "ocean navy." For strength. A power name. My little brother, age three, was Haibing, meaning "ocean coast." For a beautiful thing. I, eight, was Haiyan. That is a bird flying over the ocean, a white one called a sea swallow, because Grandfather Ocean had read a book with that bird in it. I love that name. It is so pretty. I also love my other name, Jin.

Our village had only one well, and it gave little water. Very early each morning, maybe at four o'clock, people lined up for their share. But mostly we went to a far town for water. No matter where it came from, we had to boil the water before drinking it or become very sick.

About once a week, somebody went on the water trip, except in winter, when snow lay on the ground. Snow we melted for water.

Families took turns going to the water town. This year, in late spring, Diē was visiting, and he was the one going! I began begging to go too.

"Please can I go? Please, please?" I made my eyes very pleading, like a puppy's.

"No," Ma said, for I would be riding in our wagon, with a big wheel right behind me. She was afraid I would jump off before the wagon completely stopped and be crushed by the wheel.

"I will not jump off too soon," I promised. But

Ma also feared that with so many people in the far town, I would get lost. Diē would be filling a big water tank. He could not watch me.

Then *I* worried Haijun would get to go because he was a boy. "If you let me go, I will work the bellows to keep your cook fire going," I told Ma. A very hot job. I held her hands, swinging them back and forth. "I will even watch my brothers tonight." Then I would have to carry Haibing a lot. So heavy. Ma knew that I did not like to do that.

At last she said, "Yes." I danced all around and hugged her hard, hard. I was going on a water trip! I was going on an adventure!

WATER ADVENTURE

That night I could not sleep from excitement. I had never seen a town—or anything outside our village.

Each morning the roosters start screaming, early, early, and wake you up. But *this* morning I was awake *before* the roosters.

Ma served us breakfast, her hair in a braid. As she moved, I saw her hands, swollen from hard work. Diē and I ate a soup of buckwheat noodles and potatoes, the same as we did every day. Diē was very tall, very thin. I watched him now, his gold front teeth shining, his thick eyebrows dancing, as he ate.

Then he hitched our horse to our wagon and loaded it with a huge metal tank for the water we would bring back. We did not take food with us because we were full of noodles.

Diē sat on one side of the tank. I was so excited, I nearly flew to sit on the other side. I felt grown up because I was in front with Diē.

Ma waved and called out many warnings—"Be careful! Do not fall out! Do not let your shoes fall off!"—until we were out of sight. She made our shoes. Each pair took more than one week. She did not want to make me new ones.

All morning we bumped along the uneven path, crossing hill after hill after hill. Wider and wider, into the distance, the world opened up before me, so full of surprises.

Through the wild land we sang a song to the blue sky and the pretty clouds, loud, loud. *Here is the spring!* went the words. *The flowers are blooming! The birds have new clothing!* Words about good things coming after the hard snow time.

Each new butterfly, each new flower we passed, I waved at because I was so happy. The whole time, I was looking everywhere, hoping to see wild donkeys—maybe even a wolf!

Suddenly Diē whispered, "There! A fox!"

"Where is it? Where? Where?" I started screaming, for I had never seen one.

"Shush, Daughter," Diē hushed me. "You will scare it away."

He stopped the wagon and helped me stand

very slowly to see it. I looked all around. Then—
so hard to believe!—I was looking at a fox. And a
fox was looking at me!

The water town was a mud village just like ours, but bigger. I was not disappointed, because, being a place with water, it had so much grass. So many trees. I wished I could live there, to climb those trees.

We went right away to the well. Luckily, there was no line of people waiting there.

Diē stopped the wagon and we got down. I was curious about everything. I was especially eager

to see inside this well full of water, for our village well was always almost dry. I begged Diē to let me look at the shining water.

"Do not go close without me," he warned. People, mostly children, sometimes fell into wells and drowned. So I tiptoed near it, with him right there. My heart thumping, I lay on my belly and grabbed the sides of the opening. Diē held on to my feet so I could creep close to peer in. I looked down, deep down.

Because I was born naughty, I dropped from my pocket one small stone—*plink!*—to hear the sound. Diē said, "No more stones. They make the water dirty."

From inside the cool well came a new sound. Like music. A shimmering echo. The very voice of the well.

"Thank you, little well," I said, "for letting me look into your belly."

Now, while I watched, Diē went to work. He lowered our bucket on a rope and filled it. Then he hauled it up and set it on the wagon seat, climbed on top of the wagon, and poured the water into our big tank. Up and down, up and down. Bucket after heavy bucket. It took a long time. When our tank was full, he rested a little. Then we turned for home.

On the way back, I sang even louder than before.

In our village, while Diē poured out the last drop of water for waiting families, I ran to tell Ma and my brothers all that had happened.

At night we had only kerosene lamps for light. But we did not use those much, because kerosene cost a lot. When the dark was coming, I had to eat my food fast before I could not see it.

On this night, I ate fast. Like always. Soon our house was black, black. There was nothing else to do but say good night, then sleep and dream about the wonderful fox, the wonderful singing with Diē, the wonderful well, and our wonderful trip together.

THE WILDNESS OF WIND

Most of the year, wind came howling like a wolf through our village. So fierce and so strong, sometimes it picked up lambs and other small animals. It was dangerous for young and old people. There were no trees near to hold on to. Often I had to walk backward against the wind to breathe.

It screamed loud, loud. I wanted to cover my ears, but if I did, I thought the wind might go into my mouth, then jump and roar inside me.

Sometimes I thought it would blow *me* away. Only in our tiny mud house did I feel safe from the wind.

Often in our village the wind made little tornadoes. People called them "small ghosts" and believed they really were. At first they were not there—then they were. Spinning, spinning, with stinging sand from the desert. So far they had attacked only grown-ups. Usually they just twisted on the side of the road, being scary.

There were so many stories about those little tornadoes and what you should do if one appeared. If you saw one, you could not point at it, or it would follow you. With certain looks you could warn people *It is behind you* or *It is over there.* You could point with your chin. Or speak, but then you would eat sand.

One day late in May I was going to see my

friends. Since Ma had one rare unbusy moment, she took time to fix my hair with a special oil so the wind would not ruin it.

Then I was jumping and singing on my way. I felt so happy, with my hair so pretty, so shiny with oil. All of a sudden—*No! No! No! No!*—from nowhere a small ghost appeared! It grabbed me and would not stop spinning and roaring around me. It tugged hard, hard, trying to pick me up. I thought I was done for.

I did not scream, because sand would get into my mouth. I did not move, because the small ghost would follow me. Eyes closed, I just froze. I told it, *Please go away! Please go away!* Maybe because I said *please,* after a very frightening moment the small ghost vanished.

My oily hair was now sand hair. My face was a sand face. There was sand in my eyelashes, eyebrows, nose, mouth, ears. Just everywhere.

I was so mad, I ran home for Ma to help me get clean. I had no mirror, but I must have looked a little bit horrible because Ma saw my wild appearance and shouted, "Sand girl!" She had a hard time holding her laughter in.

Things were not all bad. In our village I became famous—the only girl to be grabbed by a small ghost. And, after that big fright, I had my very own ghost story to tell.

POTATO MOUNTAIN

Our family lived off what we grew and the animals we raised. Mostly potatoes and little shreds of chicken meat sometimes. Potatoes, potatoes, potatoes. If our crops were not big or a storm tore them up or wolves stole our animals, we would eat less. We were a skinny family. I was always a little bit hungry.

Each year near the end of May the wind decided to hold its breath. Then we could start planting. The grown-ups planted the things that had to be done just right or they would not grow. Like wheat. And the plants that gave us sesame seeds for Ma's cooking oil. My brothers and I wanted to help, but Ma would not let us plant the difficult crops. So what could we plant? Potatoes, potatoes, potatoes. We could not wreck them.

Ma told my brothers and me how to do it. We cut last year's leftover potatoes into hunks. Each hunk had one or more eyes, the dark spots on the potato skins. When planted, the eyes would sprout to make new potatoes.

With my hands, I dug little holes and dropped a potato hunk into each one, at least one eye up, so it would sprout.

When the sprouts were about five inches high, after maybe two months, was the perfect time to dig up some buried potato hunks. Then I called, "Brothers! Run! It is tasting time!" Nature's magic had changed the hunks inside the ground and

turned them into a treat. So delicious! So juicy!
So sweet!

As fast as I could, I dug them up, dusted the dirt
off on my shirt, and, one after another, popped
them into my mouth. My brothers and I laughed
a lot and gobbled them down. Ma did not care if
we stuffed ourselves with potato hunks. We had
planted a big amount.

In autumn, when the new potatoes were fully grown, we dug them up. Potatoes, potatoes, potatoes. A mountain of them. When the potato mountain was piled outside our house, I thought, *Here is food for us for one whole year.* Then, gently, I patted the mountain and whispered, "Thank you, potatoes, for feeding me and my family."

A WALK WITH WOLVES

Often I heard the voices of wolves in the nearby hills. Often I heard them close. All year long the wolves were looking for food because, like us, they did not have enough to eat.

Ma's worst worry was wolves. They killed our sheep and chickens. If we were not careful, she knew they could kill *us,* too.

Because we did not have a picture, Ma told us what a wolf looked like. It was huge and always gray, not different colors like dogs. Its tail hung down. A dog's was up. A wolf had lots of teeth. VERY BIG TEETH. I always thought about those teeth. On the wall, with her hands, Ma made a shadow picture of a wolf, chomping and chomping its mouth. After explaining a wolf to us, she said, "If you see that, run!"

Once I drew a picture of what I thought was a wolf. My wolf looked like this:

I did not want to be eaten by a wolf, but I *did* want to see one. I was so curious about wolves that one summer day, when Ma was napping, I went on a wolf walk. I got my brother, Haijun, to go with me. Our little brother, Haibing, wanted to come, but I said *no*! He walked too slowly.

When we were leaving, I saw a branch in the yard. Very big. Very heavy. We wolf walkers decided to drag it behind us for protection.

Ma was one thousand percent against us going very far by ourselves. So we sneaked off quietly, quietly. As soon as we were away from our house, I whispered loudly, "Go!" Haijun and I hurried as fast as we could, lugging that branch. It gave me a feeling of power as I went into wolf country.

Along the way, I looked for wolves. I was excited and scared all at once. Going to find a wolf, I felt like a hero. With nobody telling me what to do, I felt big freedom.

The day got hot. I got tired. I began thinking
about wolves and their VERY BIG TEETH. My
mind saw Ma's shadow wolf chomping, chomping.
On us. Then every little noise was a wolf. A bird
flying up made us jump. A vole darting by made
my heart thump. We got so scared, we turned
around.

Under the wide, wild sky, I began to have wide,
wild worries. That a wolf was following us. Sneak-
ing up. I thought I heard it. I *felt* it was there.

Hiding behind a bush. Or a little lump of hill. I just *knew* it was about to pounce!

Everything prickled. My hair, my neck, my skin. Suddenly I shouted, "Wolf is coming! Brother, run!" Dragging the wolf branch behind us, we ran for our lives. We ran until we did not have any breath left, and we ran still more.

After a while, no wolf got us, so we flopped down to recover.

Back home, when Ma saw us sweaty and panting—with Haijun crying—I blurted out about our adventure. She was so angry. Like a big black storm.

"You silly children! Why did you do that? A wolf could eat you!" she shouted at us.

"But we had our wolf stick," I told her proudly. Haijun and I grabbed the big branch and dragged it over to show Ma how we'd planned to whack a wolf and chase it off. But—*Oh! Oh!*—we were so small, the two of us together could not lift that branch!

Ma became too angry to even speak.

That night I dreamed about something with VERY BIG TEETH—and it was Ma.

TREE IN TROUBLE

Where I lived, we had only a few trees, and I loved them all. I thought each one was a present to me. So pretty in summer, with their gleaming leaves and their rough bark.

Those trees were a little far from our house, and I had to walk to reach them. They grew all together. Not a forest. A little group. They held out their arms to sun, wind, snow, rain, or just plain clean blue sky. They held out their arms to *me* and said, "Climb." How could I not do what the trees asked? So I climbed every one. High, high. At the top I reached up for a handful of sky.

I climbed to see into birds' nests. When I was high in a tree, I felt like *I* was a bird.

When I visited the trees, I did not tell Ma. She would have said, "DON'T." She was afraid I would fall and break my head open, like a melon. Also she worried that I would rip the pants that had taken her so long to stitch. I am not sure which worry was worse.

Climbing up a tree, I did not tear my clothes, so I thought, *So far, I am not in trouble.* But going down I was in trouble all the way. Sliding fast against the bark, that was when things got ripped.

One time I tried to hide my torn clothes by covering them with my hands. Right away, Ma knew what was wrong. Before she could get mad, I quickly said, "That tree is in trouble. It ruined my pants. Look!" I showed her the holes.

"The tree did not climb—*you* did!" Ma shouted. "You are a girl! Be like a girl! Girls belong on the ground, not in the air!"

For punishment I had to do extra work. Like helping with the cooking. Or cleaning up. Or shoveling the dung from the animal pen. The work was worth it. I got to climb a tree.

After that, I told myself, *You will resist trees. You will stay on the ground.* I tried for a little bit, but my feet took me to trees.

Sometimes I climbed trees to compete, especially with boys. Up and down, climbing without resting. Once, a big-mouthed boy named Qiqi bragged, "You girls are nothing. You cannot climb trees. I am fastest. I am best."

Before I could stop them, the words just jumped from my mouth. "Let's see."

Now I *had* to climb. Of course I would rip my

clothes. Of course I would be in trouble.

That time, about ten of us competed, mostly boys. When somebody shouted, "Go!" we were off.

My tree was tall and the wind was screaming and the tree was swaying and I was trembling. But I just held on tight and kept going, up, up, up. My hands got red and hurt a lot. But I beat everybody!

Jumping up and down, my friends shouted, "Jin is better than you!" Qiqi made a sour face and stomped away. In that moment I think I was a hero—a little bit. But I would not be a hero to Ma, for my clothes were ripped.

When everybody else had gone and the wind had calmed itself down, I climbed the tree again, to be alone. Then I was part of the clouds. Part of the wide blue sky.

From the treetop I saw my own tiny mud house. It looked just like the rest, but it was *my* house, with my family warm inside.

I stayed in the tree for a long time, thinking of how Ma would punish me. Then the smoke from our chimney told me she was starting to cook dinner. I should help.

I went down and walked back to my home. I was happy about beating the boys. But that tree was in trouble, and so was I—again.

I burst into our house, jumping and shouting,

"Guess what? A great thing!"

"What is great?" asked Ma, seeing my torn clothing.

"I beat all the boys at tree climbing!"

For a moment everything got quiet. I waited for sharp words to come.

"That *is* great," Ma said. She smiled and patted my head. She was so proud of me! I had proved girls were better than boys.

That was the only time Ma did not punish me for climbing trees.

WINGS

Butterflies, beetles, all flying creatures—I wanted to have wings like them. To fly above my home, to see things I could not see from below. But most of all I wanted to soar the sky like an eagle.

Sometimes I wondered, *Why can they fly and I cannot?*

I walked on the ground slowly. Eagles could cross the whole sky fast. I was small. They seemed huge. I thought they were something more than birds. Things of majesty, sky kings, that flew so high, where there was mystery.

They did not flap like regular birds. They were too great for that. They just glided across the sky on their wonderful wide wings. Usually they did not make a sound. Floating along alone, they brought quiet with them.

Eagles were rulers of the high places, the wild blue spaces that nobody else had seen. They knew things I did not know. I wanted to know those things too.

I did not see many eagles, but when I did, I kept my eyes on them. I could not stop. Chin up, watching for a long time, I was not me anymore. I *was* an eagle, very wild, very free. I lifted my arms like wings and moved in wide circles. I moved over the ground, but in my heart I flew.

BIG RAIN, SMALL RAIN

In summer, sometimes I smelled a good earth smell, a smell so promising. Then I knew that a storm was coming. I was happy, for our plantings needed rain. But I was also worried. Storms were scary.

One afternoon, when I was out playing, I saw dark clouds pouring themselves over our hills. Almost at once, the sky turned from blue to blue-black. I felt the wind, stronger and stronger. I heard it start to scream. Then I really, *really* ran, before the heavy drops began to beat down, each one like a big, wet hand slapping my head.

I loved storms, but I was terrified of lightning. Often in our village it flared down chimneys, killing people. Now, as I ran, in a terrible brightness lightning blazed, and I felt the ground shake. Close after, thunder growled, dark and angry. I thought the sky would fall in pieces on top of me.

I was soaked when I sloshed into my house. There I crouched with my family like a trembling mouse, waiting for lightning to blaze down our chimney. Blown by the wild wind, rain washed our windows in all directions, up, down, every which way. Those windows, a few glass and one of hemp and paper, could not keep rain out in a storm like this.

Ma always carried a big knife, the strongest

one, the shiniest. With no rust, so it had powerful energy. When a storm came pounding down—the one that wanted to wash us away along with the new plants that did not yet have roots, and leave us hungry—Ma rushed into action.

She splashed out into our yard in her sandals. Ears plugged against the thunder, my brothers and I watched from inside as she stuck her knife into the wet earth and left it there. In a loud voice Ma told the sky, "Stop it! We do not need so much rain right now!" When the storm did not calm down, Ma stabbed the ground again.

Soon the storm did what Ma said. I was never certain why. But for a thousand thousand years, I think, Chinese people have been stabbing the earth with knives. For a thousand thousand years, huge storms have been calmed by this. Maybe from all the energy of those stabbings and all the

shouts of "Stop!" the storms know to calm down. Maybe they say to themselves, "Okay, that's it. I quit."

By now the lightning had gone. But with the big rain still raging outside, inside there came a small rain. In corners, on the bed, through the windows, in secret places we had to find, our tiny house was leaking.

Our dirt floor became mud. My brothers and I scrambled around our dripping house, placing buckets and pails and pots and pans all over, their small mouths wide open to catch the small rain.

"There's one, Brother!" "Over there, Sister!" Above the roar of wind and rain, we shouted to each other when new leaks sneaked in.

During some storms, I was supposed to be asleep in our bed ringed with rain-catcher pots. Instead I stayed wide awake listening to the *plop,*

plop of raindrops falling into the pots. Listening to the song of the rain.

When the rain had gone, the sky was like blue glass. Everything smelled clean, as if the earth was new again.

The storm gave us a rain river, rushing, rushing. Shiny with stones. It was not always in the same place, but close to our house. Right away I took a bag, went out, and found it. I crouched beside the river to see all the stones it rolled along. Green, pink, yellow, red, orange, purple. Even white and really, really black. A rainbow of stones.

I stayed there for a long time, watching the beautiful stones tumbling over each other, mumbling watery words as they must have since forever, until my legs got numb and hunger grabbed my belly. I filled my bag with them. Walking home, I listened hard, and I almost understood, in the after-storm stillness, the ancient words of the rainbow stones.

Now something else came—a *real* rainbow, reaching over our hills. A bridge of colors. Pure beauty. Like good luck was blessing my land and my village and my family and me.

GIFT FROM THE STORM

That night, after the storm, so magically, mushrooms began growing in our hills. Mushrooms! A gift from the storm. Knowing this, I stayed awake for a long time, in my mind seeing them grow.

I could not wait for the next morning to beat my friends, especially my best friend, Yinlan, to the mushroom hills. To collect the most mushrooms.

"Mushroom morning! Mushroom morning!"

I sang before the sun rose. I hugged Ma and spun her around in a silly dance. Ma loved mushroom mornings too. Mushrooms made our meals special. I was her best—and only—mushroom finder. So she was happy to dance with me.

I ate my morning noodles with Ma. But as soon as I could, I grabbed a basket Grandfather Ocean had made for me and a little hand shovel. I dashed away so fast, I was first to the mushroom place.

For mushroom gathering you must have patience. Mushrooms do not just shout, "Open your eyes! I am here!" You need to find where they are growing. It takes a long, long time.

About mushrooms, when you find them, you must pick off the small bugs. Also leave the ones with funny shapes. Mostly, you do not want those that have been above the ground too long. They look at you and say, "Leave me alone. I am old and squishy. I will not taste good."

So I went for the baby mushrooms, the ones barely bulging up from the earth. The ones you have to dig to find. When I saw them, my eyes got wide, like I was seeing gold.

I collected the baby mushrooms fast, fast. But then my friends appeared. By digging the earth up just so, I tried to fool them—mostly Yinlan—into

thinking baby mushrooms were there when they were not. Yinlan did the same to me.

We laughed and laughed when we fooled each other. My friends and I were so happy, squealing and shrieking and tricking each other and digging for mushrooms. We all went home with many mushrooms, but I found the most.

At home, with needles and strong thread, Ma and I strung some of the mushrooms and hung them out to dry. In winter they would bring big flavor to our meals.

That night Ma cooked some mushrooms. She melted pork fat in her huge cooking pot, then added potatoes and our storm gift, my mushrooms, cut into pieces.

Then Ma and my brothers ate—but I did not. Mushrooms. I loved the big excitement of finding them, but I would not eat the cooked ones. So soft and slimy, they tasted funny. Ma gave me something else. While she and my brothers enjoyed funny-tasting mushrooms, I enjoyed a plate of my favorite food—chicken feet.

THE POPCORN MAN

One day in autumn, the first snow was on the ground. Because it was so cold and windy, Ma and my brothers and I all stayed inside our tiny mud house, playing games with sheep knee bones. Suddenly, a sound shivered through the air—*BONGGGGG!* A gong.

"He's here! He's here!" I shouted. "The popcorn man!"

When that gong spoke—like magic—children would appear from everywhere, squealing and shrieking and running as fast as they could, for popcorn.

My brothers and I began shrieking too. This was the last time of the year we could have fun and a special treat before fierce winter came.

"Calm down," Ma said, but of course we could not. So she gave us money and we were off. We were all rushing to get out of our house, so we ran into each other and got stuck for a moment at the door.

Our animals started running around in the yard, baaing and braying. The guard dog started barking.

We dashed to the wide place in the path where the popcorn man had set up all the things he had brought on his bicycle. Wood for the fire, pots of corn kernels, his big gong, and, most important of all, his ancient popcorn machine.

When his fire was roaring, the popcorn man

dragged the big, heavy popcorn machine on top of it.

He was skinny like a string, and he wore only black—even his dog-skin hat was black. When he smiled, which was a lot, his face wrinkled up like an old, old one.

Waiting for our turn, my brothers and I jumped up and down, like kernels about to pop.

Everybody who wanted popcorn brought something to carry it home in. A pot, a bowl, a pan. Even our pockets. I asked for popcorn with sugar on it. I loved the crunch, but mostly I loved the sweetness.

The popcorn man measured out the corn kernels that each family wanted. Then the fun began. There was a secret button somewhere on the popcorn machine. When he pushed it, the machine began turning, toasting the kernels. As they got hot, I could hear them starting up. *Pip, pip.*

We began guessing how many seconds the popcorn would take to cook.

"Ten seconds!" I shouted, hands over my ears. Somebody else hollered, "Twenty seconds!" Another one yelled, "Twelve!" Waiting for what we knew would happen soon, my friend Yinlan and I hugged each other in delicious fear, screaming, "It's coming! It's coming!" Then, *BOOM!* A big explosion came. The popcorn was done.

A popcorn smell filled the air. So delicious. I breathed deep, deep to fill myself up with it.

The popcorn man loved to fool us, and sometimes, eyes sparkling, without warning he pushed the secret button. *BOOM!* Then we *really* shrieked—and the popcorn man *really* laughed.

Each family's corn was popped separately, so there were lots of booms! Each explosion got the dogs barking and the kids screaming. Even some grown-ups.

The popcorn machine was old and rickety, like the popcorn man's bicycle. So, often, like tiny white shooting stars, popcorn flew out from the broken places. All of us rushed to grab it. And—do not worry—nothing was left on the ground.

When it was Yinlan's turn, a big breath of wind picked up the popcorn and blew it away. "My popcorn!" she cried. We all looked up and watched that popcorn cloud fly.

"It is okay, Yinlan," I said. "We have lots." And I shared some of ours with her.

When the popcorn was popped and the pots and pans and pockets were full, the popcorn man smothered his fire, packed his things on his bicycle, and rode away. My brothers and I waved and waved until he was gone. Then, covering our pot from the greedy wind, we walked home to eat popcorn with Ma.

SCREAMING CHALK AND SMOKE, SMOKE, SMOKE

That year, in September, I started school, and I loved it. I wanted to know everything there was to know. But also I hoped for days when something different would happen, apart from our usual lessons.

My school had one room, with students ages eight to thirteen, all in the same class. Because I was eight, I could go. My brothers stayed home. They were too young.

My teacher, Mr. Chen, was very tall, very

skinny, and very, very kind. He talked fast. He had only one suit, blue with a Mao collar, so he always wore that, along with a round black hat. He taught every subject—Mandarin, Chinese history, geography, math, reading. He was also the principal and did the other jobs too. My teacher, he ran the school.

Mr. Chen always told us, "Anything you can learn, learn. It will not make you heavy. It will lift you up."

If we were not good—maybe if we talked when he was talking—he made a sound like chalk screaming on the blackboard. If we were still not quiet, he said, "I will do that again—but louder."

In the cold months it was about four degrees below zero outside, so there was always a fire in the schoolroom stove to keep us a little bit warm. Every year each family had to bring thirty-five pounds of straw to start the fire and fifty pounds of dung to keep it going, or their children could not go to school.

Each school day, a different team of students started the fire before the rest of us came.

One early morning, when we opened the classroom door, we met nothing but freezing cold and smoke, smoke, smoke. So thick we could not see each other! Everybody began coughing and crying from the stinging smoke.

"Somebody open a window! Leave the door open!" Mr. Chen shouted. "Move the benches and tables!"

When the smoke had thinned, what a mess! Charred straw was all over the place. To build the fire, the team had put straw first into the stove, then dung, and lit it. It kept going out. The kids thought the straw was the problem. They kept tossing it to the mud floor again and again, rebuilding the fire with fresh straw and the old dung. They could not tell from holding it that the *dung* was wet inside! From the heat, water in

the dung dripped down, smothering the fire and making smoke.

Smoke tears ran down the fire makers' faces, leaving lines like little rivers. Their cheeks were smeared from rubbing away the tears with their hands, black from the burnt straw. I called them smoke people.

"You should see your faces!" We laughed. But they did not care. They laughed too.

Still coughing and choking and wiping away smoke tears, everybody helped fix the fire and clean up our classroom.

Mr. Chen was not mad. He knew the team had been working hard to get the fire going. Instead of a book lesson, we had a fire class.

"The most important thing you need for a fire is *dry dung*," he said. "And you can only tell which is dry from the weight. Always choose the light dung, not the heavy."

At school, I hoped for days when something different would happen, apart from our usual lessons. This time I got my wish.

BLACK JUICE

One subject Mr. Chen did not teach was calligraphy, fancy writing passed down through the centuries from our old, old generations.

Some people make calligraphy with a special pen. We used a special paintbrush and "black juice"—ink. The black juice was precious. Very expensive. In a one-room school with excited children packed close together, there was a big danger of it spilling. So black juice was not allowed at school. I learned calligraphy at home.

Ma's father, Grandfather Wang, was an artist. He lived far from us, so he told Diē to teach me calligraphy whenever he could leave his job to visit us. Even if Ma had known calligraphy, which she did not, she was much too busy to teach it.

Diē put a table on the bed for me to work on, then placed a thin piece of paper over the page of a book. With a paintbrush and black juice, I tried to trace the characters. Each one stood for something—maybe sky, cat, fish.

Every day when Diē was home, I worked on calligraphy. I had to sit there *so* still and not move, or I might spill the black juice and spoil my work.

Calligraphy was difficult and I did not love it. It was hard for me, only eight years old, even to hold the paintbrush. It had to be held not at an angle, but straight up. Diē steadied the top of it because I was not strong enough.

And, *oh,* the black juice! What a big stink! Like dung. Sometimes one of my hands would hold the paintbrush while the other held my nose. "No," Diē told me. "One hand must hold the paper. You have to do calligraphy with the bad smell."

One day, suddenly, an idea came shining into my head. My classroom walls were blank. They had no decorations. No drawings, no maps, nothing.

So excited, I said to Diē, "My classroom is ugly. I want to make it pretty. Will you help?"

"Of course, Daughter," he said. "What can I do?"

"Teach me a calligraphy character that will make our room beautiful."

Diē asked, "Which one?"

I thought about what Mr. Chen and my schoolmates would want. Because they lived in this dry place, to see the big ocean water was their dream, just like Grandfather Ocean's. And mine.

"I want to paint the ocean," I told Diē.

He showed me what the ocean charac-ter looked like. I worked hard, hard to make it perfect. Calligraphy was no longer a job to do. It was a way for me to brighten my school.

When I was ready to make the final painting, I asked Diē for a big piece of paper. "I want to paint my ocean *big, big.* So that everybody at school can see it."

I walked to school one morning with my calligraphy rolled up carefully. I hugged it close—but not tight enough to crush it—to keep that robber, wind, from stealing it.

Right away I handed my work to Mr. Chen.

"What is this?" he asked.

My face felt warm from shyness. I said, "A gift."

My heart felt tight. Would my classmates be amazed or think my work was nothing?

Before, the class had been talking, talking, talking. But when Mr. Chen unrolled my calligraphy, the room got quiet. Everybody's eyes grew wide.

I told them, "This means 'ocean.'"

Then he pinned my calligraphy to a bare wall. I think the wall felt happy.

With one hand raised toward my work, Mr. Chen said, "Look, class. A wonderful thing. Jin has given us the ocean."

FAMILY PORTRAIT

Some years we got our picture taken. For us, especially Ma, that was a big, big thing.

We never knew when the photographer was coming. For payment he accepted only money. No eggs or other trades like our tiny store took.

One day he walked into our house carrying his shiny black camera.

"Do you want your portrait taken?" he asked Ma.

"Yes," said Ma eagerly. Of course, she was

already worrying, I think, about getting us to look nice.

"I will wait outside while you get ready," he said. He stopped at all the houses, so he had a whole day of taking photographs. But mostly of waiting.

Right away Ma jumped into action. First she cut our hair and washed it. In a big rush, she scrubbed mine so hard, my head hurt. I was so happy to be having my picture taken, I did not care. Then she tied ribbons in my hair, in the shapes of butterflies, to make me pretty. My brothers' hair was too short. They could not be made pretty.

It was winter, so we wore many layers of clothing. Ma hurried to find our newest clothes. Tug, tug, she pulled them over our heads, on top of the dirty old ones. My kind-of-new shirt

already had a hole in it. "No holes!" cried Ma. She pulled it off me and tugged another shirt on.

When we were ready, Ma gave us her most serious face and commanded, "Do not wrinkle your clothes!"

Grandfather Ocean was with us this day. We sat on the bed, on his bony lap, and tried not to wrinkle our clothes. But we kept squirming and squeezing each other for the best place to sit on him.

"Do not move! Just sit!" Ma shouted in a fluster. But we kept jumping on and off Grandfather Ocean's lap, we were so excited.

It was a very cold and windy day. So, while the photographer waited, Ma cleaned our noses every two minutes. With tough notebook paper, so painful. We had no tissues. But runny noses would spoil the picture. When we wiped our noses on our clothes, she screeched, "DO NOT DO THAT!"

She rushed from child to child, because after she cleaned one nose, the next one was running. "Do not let your noses run!" Ma shouted over and over. Of course, we did anyway. We could not help it.

Our faces were red from the cold, so Ma scrubbed them to make the red go away. Then they got redder.

When the photographer came in, my little brother was afraid of him and all the commotion. He kept crying and running away. We kept having to catch him. All but Grandfather Ocean.

"You have to smile!" Ma told Haibing over and over.

I said, "Calm down. Do not cry. This picture is not painful."

But that little one did not listen.

Finally, Ma said, "Smile! Smile!" and began tickling him. Even though he was still crying, he smiled. The camera went *click!* And that was it.

After about one month, the photographer brought our picture. There were our runny-nosed selves, looking out at us. Ma leaned the portrait against a wall and said in an angry voice, "Shame on you! You let your noses run!" But behind those hard words, I knew she was smiling.

TINY HOUSE IN WINTER

Outside our tiny house, one winter day, snow was falling down. Usually, I loved to go out, to see the icicles' teeth along the windows, our pretty chickens roosting on the sill beneath them. But this day, because it was too snowy to see, our family had to stay inside, squeezed into our one tiny room.

Of course, we banged into each other a lot. Often our heads—and other parts—got big bumps.

Haijun and I had brought the newest lambs into the house to keep them from freezing. They began baaing at being separated from their mothers. Outside, their mothers were baaing to say, "Come back!"

The lambs ran all over the room, baaing. Haijun ran all over too, laughing. He began poking me when he ran by. Poking, poking.

"Slow down!" Ma shouted above the noise.

"Stop!" I shrieked, but Haijun kept poking me, not listening to Ma at all. Once, I forgot to dodge, and he hit me with his head and I got a nosebleed. HIS BIG HARD HEAD. The hardest in the world.

"Sorry, Sister!" he shouted, and kept running.

"Look out for the lambs!" Ma shouted at him, while trying to keep my blood from dripping onto the floor. My smaller brother, Haibing, was crying because I was crying.

Finally, Haijun stopped running and tried to ride a lamb.

"NO!" Ma yelled at her loudest. "You will hurt it!"

So instead he poked me again. Then I went after *him*.

Such a big confusion.

Things got worse. Ma began washing our clothes in melted snow. Inside the house. When they were clean, they were dripping wet. She had to hang them outside so the dirt floor did not become mud.

Of course, when Ma hung up the wet clothes, they froze. There they were on the line, shirts and pants, sleeves straight out, legs straight out. So cold. So stiff. Like bodies with no people.

Late that afternoon Ma suddenly jumped up. "The clothes!" she cried. She had to bring them in before the fierce winds began howling, howling like huge white wolves and blew them away.

We three crawled onto the bed, carrying the lambs, so Ma could hang the frozen clothes over some little stools close to the fire. The stools did not fit into the room when all of us were running around.

That night, while we were sleeping, now and then Ma turned the clothes over, to dry better. Then she dozed off—until a bad smell woke her up. "The clothes!" she cried again. Our clothes were burning a little bit.

Ma grabbed them away from the fire and stomped out the sparks, but her shout woke us up. The lambs began baaing from hunger. So Ma and I chewed bread into the tiniest pieces and fed them. Haijun refused to chew bread for lambs. He thought it was not a good thing for a boy with a power name. Little Haibing chewed the bread, then, smiling wide, swallowed it.

I watched my brother eating the lambs' food. I felt my hurt nose. I saw our smoking clothing.

Tears began to fill my eyes. But suddenly— I laughed. Then we were all laughing, my family and I. What else could we do? In our tiny house, one winter night, when snow was falling down.

THE TASTE OF WINTER

One day, warm for winter, I went out to watch the melting snow dripping onto the handle of our door. The water stayed there. Shiny, like ice. Very pretty. I wanted to taste it. I wanted to know the taste of winter. So I licked it. Then—uh-oh!—I could not get my tongue back into my mouth. It was frozen to the door!

Somehow I screamed even though my tongue was stuck. I was hugging the open door and crying because my tongue hurt—and because I was very scared.

No neighbors came. They were used to children crying and screaming. But my brothers ran to my rescue and began crying too, saying, "Sister, Sister, are you hurting?" and trying to pull me off the door. That made everything worse, and I cried more.

Finally, Ma was there. But it took her a while to warm snow and pour it on the handle to release my tongue.

My tongue was numb, and it took some time for my family to understand my words. I thought, *I cannot speak. My tongue is not there!*

Ma yelled at my brothers, "Be careful! Nobody lick that handle!" Then she added, "If your hands are wet, they will stick too! Nobody touch that handle!" So angry, she said to me, "If you do that again, your tongue will be gone! Then you can only make a noise—AAAAGH!"

BRICKS AND LOVE

To me, skating was like flying. I went fast and felt light, like I might lift off the earth. In our village we skated on the dirty water that people had thrown out. When they tossed it onto the path, it froze. A perfect skating place.

My skates were Ma's old summer shoes, too big for me and with no tread left on the soles. Those shoes were very good for skating. They slid so nicely on the ice.

One winter day I was on my way to skate.

I was wearing almost all my clothes against the cold, with many scarves wrapped around my head.

With Ma's slippery shoes on, I had to walk slowly, carefully, not to fall down. I was wobbling on my way, happy because all around me the world was so white, so pretty.

Suddenly I heard loud barking. Some boys were throwing things at three big dogs. The dogs were very angry.

When the boys ran away, the dogs rushed at me. I tried to hide, but there was no place to go.

These were home dogs, but not the sweet ones. Trouble dogs. The ones that would completely eat you if they could. They were wild like wolves, and the sound they made was low and terrifying. They wanted to bite and bite a lot.

The dogs knocked me down and began biting every place. My head, my legs, my arms. The only thing they did not bite was Ma's shoes. The pain was like eight thousand angry ants inside my heart.

Then the dogs' owner burst from his house, shouting and shaking a stick at them. He scared them away and carried me home.

Our neighbors began talking about the "dog disease," rabies. There was no cure, everybody said. Ma was scared. My brothers were scared. I was scared completely. What if I got the dog disease and died terribly?

Our village had no doctor, so Ma took over. She knew that with dog bites you could not wait. She had to fix me right then.

Ma had heard about a cure the old people used—bricks. Bricks were the thing to suck out "dog poison." Not old, dirty ones. New bricks only.

Luckily, neighbors were building a brick

house. The dog owner brought some of those bricks to Ma. She put one on each of my wounds. At first the blood that they sucked out was black. Little by little it got redder. When each brick was very bloodied—every one or two hours—Ma put on a new one. Again, again, again. Bricks were all around the bed, so she just grabbed new ones from the pile.

My friends did not visit me, they were so afraid of getting sick, but my brothers were good to me then. They held my hands all the time. "The village people are waiting for you to die," Haijun told me. "But do not worry, Sister. You will be fine."

At our tiny store, Ma spent extra money to buy special foods, like canned pineapple. In case I did die, she wanted me to eat delicious things first.

When she could, Ma sat with me and told me what a good girl I was.

Even though the cure was not done, right

away I wanted to get up and go outside.

"Now can I go out?" I asked each time Ma changed a brick.

Each time, Ma would shout, "No! Do not move or the dog poison will kill you!"

She forced me to lie still for about a week.

Brick by brick Ma cured me. It took a long time—a month, maybe—for me to fully recover. With bricks and love, that is how Ma kept me alive.

GOOD FORTUNE

Before the old year became the new one, there were a thousand things to be done. So that the new year would be better than the old one, the whole family had to have haircuts and baths. They had to also have new clothes and new boots. To make these things, Ma started working at least two months before the most important time, New Year's Eve.

Each year we took turns for whose clothing and boots Ma made first. This year, at last my turn came, and she gave me my first boot. The second one was not ready.

I grabbed my new boot and hugged it and put it on. Wearing one new boot and one old one, I ran through the snow to Yinlan's house. "Look!" I said. "Ma is making my boots!" Then I showed everybody else I knew.

This time each year Diē came home to help with the extra work. When he arrived, we grabbed him by the arms and the hands and legs, wherever we could. He could not shake us off, so he laughed and laughed. "Did you bring presents?" we asked over and over. Then he laughed more, because, of course, he had.

Apart from stitching new boots and new clothing, Ma washed everything she could get her hands on. Even the blankets. The house had

to be clean too. Inside it had to be painted white, for the good fortune of the new year to begin.

My brothers and I tried to help with painting, but we were not good at that. Ma kept saying, "Do not lean on the walls." Not meaning to, we touched them and got white paint on our hands and faces and clothes. "Do not come close to me," Diē said, because he was dripping paint everywhere. But I wanted to be close to him—he had been gone for so long.

Diē also helped with cooking. Food was the center of our New Year's celebration. Some foods had bigger importance than others, like meatballs. Round little circles, they showed that your family was together.

Another food of big importance was the dumpling. Really, it was of the highest importance. Dumplings look like old-China silver money. When you eat a dumpling, it gives you good luck, and you will have much money for certain.

It is very, very bad fortune if you make a mistake preparing dumplings. If the dough is not just right, or a dumpling opens up when it is boiling, you will lose money for certain. If you drop one on the floor, imagine what will happen! At New Year's time children were never allowed to touch them—or even go near them. We could help clean carrots and cabbages, but that was it. Even to Diē, Ma said many times, "Be careful! Do not drop the dumplings!"

Apart from ten other not-so-dangerous dishes, my parents made hundreds of meatballs and dumplings. In five or six of the dumplings, Ma hid silver coins—for good fortune, of course. She knew which ones had coins inside, because she added a little mouse tail of dough to them. Ma always gave those mouse-tail dumplings to Haibing. I never got any. That Haibing, he was even more spoiled than the new little lambs Ma and I chewed bread for!

These days, in my mind I sent everything bad out the window—bad luck, bad health, bad crops, bad weather, too little water, and, of big importance for me, bad grades.

I thought, *All the good luck is coming.* I wanted

to help luck come. Red means luck, so I cut lots of red paper into shapes—flowers and birds and butterflies—and put them all over the house. Finally, Ma said, "That is enough." *The more red paper, the more good fortune,* I thought, so I said, "You can never have enough."

On New Year's Eve, the lamps were lit to burn until dawn. To bring a new year of light. Diē and Grandfather Ocean built a big fire in our yard but did not light it. Not yet.

While my parents were preparing dinner, my brothers and I sat on Grandfather Ocean's lap, and he told us the story of Nian the monster. "Thousands of years ago," said Grandfather Ocean, "that Terrible One came on New Year's Eve to eat people, mostly children. Each year he comes back.

"Nian is afraid of fire," Grandfather Ocean went on. "So people set off firecrackers, build big fires in their yards, and wear red clothing. When you run in your red things, Nian thinks you *are* fire and is scared off.

"Nian has not been seen for thousands of years. But, just in case, right at midnight, we still light fires. A little bit to scare him away, but mostly to welcome the New Year—and, of course, to keep warm."

When the story was over, we enjoyed our feast. I tried a taste of each of the foods, but mostly I ate dumplings.

After dinner we were allowed to wear our new clothes. I rushed to put on my pretty things. I could hardly sit still from excitement.

But now came the hard part—waiting for midnight, the time when the old year turned. In what seemed like longer than forever, I fidgeted and bothered my brothers until—at last—midnight came. Fire time!

In a rush we all went outside. While my brothers and I ran shrieking in our red clothing, Diē and Grandfather Ocean lit the fire they had built before. They lit strings and strings of firecrackers. The fire roared. The firecrackers crackled and popped. A beautiful noise.

At the same time came more beautiful noise— throughout our village, children running and shrieking, fires roaring, and firecrackers popping and crackling!

Ma had still not finished my second boot, so I wore my old one again. Then I ran to join my friends. Even though it was deep winter, I did not hear the voices of wolves. Because my friends and I were making so much noise, I heard only the voices of happiness.

Carrying paper lanterns we had made ourselves, we dashed to the neighbors' houses. We laughed and were so loud, our neighbors knew we were coming. They gave us sunflower seeds, candy, and walnuts. Sometimes even peanuts. Ma had stitched many big pockets onto my clothes to hold these gifts. Then, through the silent snow, I walked along with my friends, eating my treats and laughing the New Year in.

The lamps were still glowing when I got home. I hugged each one of my family. "Good fortune," I wished them, for the year to come. I put my new boot beside my pillow and looked around the room. I saw my tiny mud house, my mother, my father, and my brothers. In a house so close was my Grandfather Ocean. I knew then I did not have to hope for it. I already had good fortune.

AUTHORS' NOTES

I am Jin from the tiny mud house in the village of Nan Ba Zi, in the province of Inner Mongolia, China. This book takes place in 1982, when I was eight.

Our family spoke our village language, which has no name. The words in our language and in Mandarin are exactly the same, but they are pronounced differently.

After living in Nan Ba Zi for eleven years, I moved with my family to Shanxi Province. When I was fifteen, we got our first house with running water and electricity. I no longer had to rush to finish dinner before dark came! I could drink water whenever I wanted to! At first I drank it all the time, because I felt like the water might run away.

Following middle school, I attended and graduated from a three-year cultural school. It offered film, art, music, dance, drama. Everything together. I learned to play piano from a schoolmate and every day sneaked into the music room to practice. I also learned traditional dances of the world and got a dancing job near Shanghai. I love dance because it represents how much beauty there is in life.

Even though I knew few words of English, at the age of thirty-five, magically, I somehow got myself to the United States! I needed to survive by teaching yoga, so I learned English on YouTube. I practiced so hard each day my jaw was sore. But my brain would not quit. I kept repeating yoga words—like *workout*—nonstop.

Also by magic, Tony Johnston became my yoga student. Her curiosity, kindness, and questions sparked memories of my childhood. She suggested we write a book about those days—this book, the one you are holding.

In 2019, I went back to my old home. When my feet first touched the dirt path, the smell of my village hugged me.

The very smell of my childhood. My house seemed a little tinier. Everywhere I turned, there was a wall. How could we have lived in so small a place?

I do not regret one moment of my life in Nan Ba Zi. I did not know our life was hard. I had so much fun with my friends, so much freedom. Those were my happiest times.

My village, my tiny mud house, my family—especially my hero mom—made me strong. They made me who I am.

In the spring of 1999, at last I saw the ocean. It lies to the east of the Hebei Province of China and is called the Bohai Sea. I was so excited to be there, living my dream. I had wondered what I should wear to this wonderful place. So for this I wore a long dress. It was very windy, and the wind caught my dress as I danced and danced in the sand. In a small boat, I went out over this wide, shining, blue wonder. I dipped my hand into the water, and I thought about my grandfather.

- In Chinese, *Diē* is pronounced *Dian,* with the emphasis on the second syllable.
- Though I tried quite hard, I never saw a wolf in the wild.
- The New Year is our most important holiday. Recently, I found out that some people call it the Lunar New Year. To my family and our entire village, it was simply the New Year.

Jin Wang, 2024

This book began with mushrooms. Once when Jin, my yoga teacher, saw mushrooms growing in front of my house, she asked if she could eat them. "No!" I nearly shouted, because they could be poisonous. Then Jin began telling me about collecting mushrooms in China when she was young.

After that, during our yoga sessions, I asked her more about her childhood. I kept jumping up from the yoga mat, mumbling her words aloud, until I could grab a pencil to write them on a Post-it or a pen to write on my hands. Anything to get them down before they escaped. To capture her voice and her spirit.

Our yoga sessions were chopped up. The story was chopped up. So instead I began talking with Jin after yoga, writing everything she said on yellow blocks of paper as fast as I could. So many Post-its. So many yellow blocks. So many inky hands.

Jin's story touched me in a deep place. I wanted to help her share it.

Tony Johnston, 2024

ILLUSTRATOR'S NOTE

Reading Jin's story hit close to home . . . my grandparents' home! It was a mud house just like Jin's, in Darlagtu, another Inner Mongolian town. Good luck finding it on a map! I spent many months there when I was little, and heard stories about my parents' childhood. Although my family is ethnically Mongolian, Jin's story reminded me a lot of my parents' experiences, and of my own fond memories at my grandparents' house. It made me very happy to be able to share a glimpse of this world through my illustrations.

Anisi Baigude, 2024